Veterinarians

BY CECILIA MINDEN

The Child's World

Published by The Child's World®
1980 Lookout Drive • Mankato, MN 56003-1705
800-599-READ • www.childsworld.com

Acknowledgments
The Child's World®: Mary Berendes, Publishing Director
The Design Lab: Design
Jody Jensen Shaffer: Editing
Pamela J. Mitsakos: Photo Research

Photos
AlexRaths/iStock.com: cover, 1, 14; Alina555/iStock.com: 8; Bobby Flowers/Dreamstime.com : 17; kali9/iStock.com: 4, 5, 12; Monkey Business Images/Shutterstock.com: 18; Nagy-Bagoly Ilona/123RF.com: 6-7; Nenov/iStock.com: kibble; Photodisc: design elements; pick-uppath/iStock.com: 13; Robin Murphy: 9; Samuel Borges Photography/Shutterstock.com: 20-21; Vitalinka/Shutterstock.com: 22; webphotographeer/iStock.com: 10-11

ISBN 9781626870208
LCCN 2013947296

Printed in the United States of America
Mankato, MN
December, 2013
PA02191

ABOUT THE AUTHOR

Dr. Cecilia Minden is a university professor and reading specialist with classroom and administrative experience in grades K–12. She earned her PhD in reading education from the University of Virginia.

CONTENTS

Hello, My Name Is Tony.

Hello. My name is Tony. Many people live and work in my neighborhood. Each of them helps the neighborhood in different ways.

I thought of all the things I like to do. I like animals. I help take care of the pets in our house. How could I help my neighborhood when I grow up?

Kids who enjoy helping animals might make good veterinarians.

I Could Be a Veterinarian!

Veterinarians are doctors who work with animals. Animals can't tell the doctor what is hurting. A veterinarian has to put together different pieces of information to figure out what is wrong. The best part of being a veterinarian is working with animals all day long!

When Did This Job Start?
The first school of veterinary medicine opened in 1762 in Lyons, France. The first U.S. veterinary school opened one hundred years later.

Veterinarians need to be very patient and gentle.

Learn About This Neighborhood Helper!

The best way to learn is to ask questions. Words such as *who*, *what*, *where*, *when*, and *why* will help me learn about being a veterinarian.

Where Can I Learn More?
American Veterinary Medical Association
1931 N. Meacham Road, Suite 100
Schaumburg, IL 60173

Association of American
Veterinary Medical Colleges
1101 Vermont Avenue NW, Suite 301
Washington, DC 20005

Asking a veterinarian questions will help you learn more about the job.

Who Can Become a Veterinarian?

Boys and girls who are good with animals may want to become veterinarians. It is also important for veterinarians to be gentle and to have a lot of patience. They have to handle nervous or sick animals. They often must speak to worried owners.

Veterinarians help the neighborhood in many ways. Some provide care for family pets. Others examine farm animals, wildlife, and zoo animals.

Veterinarians help both zoo animals and family pets.

How Many Veterinarians Are There?
About 58,000 people work as veterinarians.

Meet a Veterinarian!

This is Dr. Robin Downing. Dr. Robin is a veterinarian in Windsor, Colorado. When she is not at her hospital, she likes to travel all over the world teaching people how to care for animals.

Dr. Robin loves helping people learn how to care for animals.

Where Can I Learn to Be a Veterinarian?

It takes a long time to become a veterinarian. Students go to a school of veterinary medicine for four years after they graduate from college. Veterinarians can choose to specialize, which means they learn a lot about one thing in particular. A veterinarian may want to work with only one animal family, such as horses or pigs.

Students must study long hours to become veterinarians.

Dr. Robin treats family pets such as dogs, cats, rabbits, rats, ferrets, and guinea pigs.

How Much School Will I Need?

Many students in veterinary school already have a four-year college degree. Most veterinary schools require at least two years of college courses. Veterinary school takes four years. Veterinarians must pass tests given by the state where they live. They are then given a license so they can work.

What Does a Veterinarian Need to Do the Job?

Dr. Robin uses many different instruments to take care of her animals. Many of these instruments are like the ones doctors use to take care of people!

Dr. Robin uses a stethoscope to listen to an animal's heart, an otoscope to look in its ears, and an ophthalmoscope to look in its eyes.

This veterinarian is listening to a dog's heart.

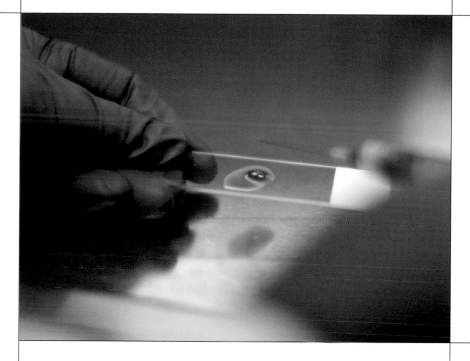

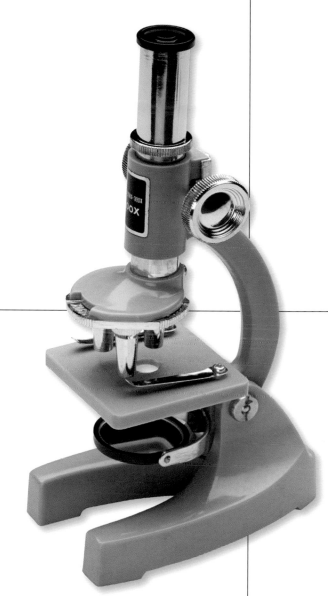

Dr. Robin uses a **microscope**. Sometimes she does a blood test on animals that are sick. Dr. Robin then places a drop of blood on a **slide**. She looks at the blood under the microscope to see what is wrong with the animal.

Microscopes help us see very tiny objects.

Where Does a Veterinarian Work?

Dr. Robin works in a hospital that looks just like a hospital for humans. The only difference is that Dr. Robin's hospital is much smaller.

Most veterinarians treat animals in an exam room.

There are exam rooms for the animals, a **laboratory** for testing blood and urine, and a **pharmacy**. There is also a surgery suite for animals that need an operation.

There are two kinds of workdays at Dr. Robin's hospital. Some days are outpatient days. Animals, or patients, come in for a visit but then go home the same day. An owner might bring a pet in for a checkup or to make sure it is getting the right medicine. Maybe the patient isn't feeling well and the owner wants the veterinarian to figure out what is wrong.

What's It Like Where I'll Work?
Veterinarians who care for pets usually work in an animal clinic or hospital. These places are clean and well-lighted, but they are often noisy. Veterinarians who treat large animals such as horses and cows usually work outdoors on a farm.

There are also workdays when surgery is performed. This is when Dr. Robin treats animals that need an operation. An owner usually arrives early in the morning and drops her pet off at the hospital. Dr. Robin and her staff check to make sure the patient is well enough to have the surgery. The animal is then given medicine so it doesn't feel any pain. Dr. Robin keeps a close eye on the patient after the surgery. She wants to make sure the animal is recovering well. The owner can usually come back for her pet the next day.

How Much Money Will I Make?
Most veterinarians make between $50,000 and $86,000 a year.

Who Works with Veterinarians?

There are many people who help Dr. Robin care for animals. A receptionist greets each owner and patient. A veterinary nurse and a veterinary technician assist Dr. Robin with medical care.

What other Jobs Might I Like?
- Animal scientist
- College teacher
- Dentist
- Medical scientist
- Physician
- Zoologist

Nurses and technicians help veterinarians care for patients.

Sometimes veterinarians help animals in emergency situations, like this rescued hedgehog. Veterinarians are always working hard to protect animals and keep them healthy.

When Is a Veterinarian an Escape Artist?

Dr. Robin once had a patient with a very unusual dog collar. This curious puppy had gotten her head stuck in a cement block. Dr. Robin and her staff gave the puppy some medicine to calm her down. They gently pushed and pulled until the puppy's head was free.

How Might My Job Change?
Most veterinarians start off working for other veterinarians. They eventually gain experience, and many go on to open their own veterinary offices. Some veterinarians even become teachers in colleges of veterinary medicine.

I Want to Be a Veterinarian!

I think being a veterinarian would be a great way to be a neighborhood helper. Someday I may be the doctor you see at the animal hospital!

Is This Job Growing?
The need for veterinarians will grow faster than other jobs.

Why Don't You Try Being a Veterinarian?

Do you think you would like to be a veterinarian? Why don't you try giving your pet a daily massage? Start at your pet's head. Slowly and gently work your hands all the way to the tail.

Maybe one day you'll be taking care of the pets in your neighborhood.

A massage will help you build a bond with your animal friend. Your hands will help you learn what your animal feels like. You should tell your veterinarian right away if you find a lump or bump that doesn't feel right!

Massage is good for animals and will help you learn about your pet's body.

GLOSSARY

laboratory (LAB-ruh-tor-ee) a room that is used for scientific research and experiments

microscope (MY-kruh-skohp) an instrument with powerful lenses that allows scientists to study very tiny objects

pharmacy (FAR-muh-see) a drugstore

slide (SLYDE) a small piece of glass that is used to view objects under a microscope

LEARN MORE ABOUT VETERINARIANS

BOOKS

Bowman-Kruhm, Mary. *A Day in the Life of a Veterinarian.* New York: PowerKids Press, 2000.

Englart, Mindi Rose. *Veterinarian.* San Diego: Blackbirch Press, 2003.

Parks, Peggy. *Veterinarian.* San Diego: Kidhaven Press, 2004.

WEB SITES

Visit our home page for lots of links about veterinarians:

www.childsworld.com/links

Note to Parents, Teachers, and Librarians: We routinely check our Web links to make sure they're safe, active sites—so encourage your readers to check them out!

INDEX